PERFECT PIE AND PASTRY RECIPES

HOMEMADE DESSERT PIES MADE EASY COOKBOOK

by Katherine Hupp

DEDICATION

Many thanks go to Jeff, Shane, Esther, Logan and Ethan Hupp
for being such willing taste testers.

I would also like to acknowledge the three women in my life
who have most influenced my pie making abilities over the
years: Grandmother Rosa Mace, Grandmother Olive Hupp and
dear friend Ginny Talbott. They are no longer here to guide
me, but I paid close attention and learned their lessons well.

CONTENTS

Introduction

Many cooks are intimidated by the thought of pie making. Some pies, especially cream and custard type pies, have the undeserved reputation of being difficult to make. This is simply not the case.

By following these recipes and using the tips located in the beginning of the book, you will soon be making delicious fruit, cream, and custard pies for your family and friends. The days of buying a barely acceptable pie from a store will be over.

When your family discovers how mouthwatering your homemade pies are, they will be begging for pie for dessert. And once you see for yourself just how easy they actually are to make, you won't mind delivering what they ask for.

In the event you find yourself out of a common ingredient used in these recipes, a short list of substitutions is located in the back of the book.

If you are new to pie making, I recommend reading the 'Tips' chapters before trying any of the recipes.

Please remember that all ovens are not the same and will vary in temperature. Your oven may require more or less time to bake the perfect pie, so be sure to keep an eye on the browning process. You don't want to accidently burn your crust or serve an undercooked pie.

Happy Pie Making!

Tips for Pastry Dough

It is fine if you feel the need to buy pre-made refrigerated pastry or frozen pie shells. In truth, there are some good tasting ones on the market today. But remember, this book is about learning to make homemade pies. You can learn to make tasty, flaky pie crusts right in your own kitchen.

1. Always use ice water in your pastry recipe.

2. If you choose a pastry recipe that calls for oil instead of shortening, be sure to chill the oil before adding it to the flour.

3. In recipes calling for shortening or butter, make sure it is cold to start. When cutting the shortening into the flour, if you see the dough starting to get shiny or having a liquid appearance, place it in the refrigerator to chill for a few minutes. Shininess means the shortening has begun to warm and melt.

4. Cut the shortening or butter into the flour until it resembles coarse meal. Think of what cornmeal looks like. You want a similar texture. You can use a pastry dough cutter to do this. If you don't have one, a wide tined fork or two knives held together work well.

5. Do not over mix your dough. I can't stress this enough! Just mix the dough until it barely sticks together. If additional water is needed, add it a few drops at a time. You should be able to

see bits of shortening or butter in the mix. Over mixing will result in a tough pie crust.

6. Roll your pastry dough on a lightly floured surface and use as few strokes of the rolling pin to shape it as you can manage. Over working the dough with a rolling pin will also result in toughness.

7. When making a pie recipe that calls for a top and bottom crust, you will need a pastry recipe for two shells. Divide the dough into balls, with one being a little larger than the other. The largest portion will be rolled out to fit the bottom of the pie pan, the smaller of the two will become the top crust.

8. Check to see if your crust is rolled out large enough to fit your pie plate. Simply turn your pie plate upside down on the rolled out dough. For the bottom crust, the dough should extend beyond the rim of the plate by about 2 inches; by 1 inch for the top crust.

9. It is easy to get the crust into proper position on the pie plate. Fold each crust in half, and then fold in half again. The crust will now be one-quarter in size, and in the shape of a wedge of pie. Place the dough with the pointy end in the center of the pan and simply fold back out. This works the same for getting both the bottom and top crusts into perfect position.

10. Trim crusts back to three-fourths of an inch before fluting the edge. To make a tight seal, turn or roll the edge of top crust underneath the lip of the bottom crust. Do this until the edges of both crusts (or single crust if you are making a one crust pie) are even with the side of the pie plate before fluting. To flute the edge, pinch and press the edges of the crust together firmly

with your fingers until you are satisfied with the appearance. It can be as simple as pinching the dough together and then pressing down lightly with one finger to make a decorative edging.

11. When pre-baking both homemade and store bought pie shells, be sure to prick the bottom and sides of pie shell with a fork. This helps keep the pie shell lying flat while baking.

12. To allow steam to vent, cut slits or prick the top of crust before placing the pie in the oven. If you wish, this is the time to make an especially attractive pie by carving a design into the top crust. It's easy to cut vine, petal and leaf shapes with a sharp knife.

Tips for Pie Making

1. Keep cooked cream and custard pies from becoming lumpy by mixing half of the hot cooked mixture into the beaten eggs. Do this instead of adding the eggs directly into the cooking pot. Stir eggs and hot mixture well and return to the pot.

2. The amount of cornstarch and egg greatly affect the thickening process of cream and custard pies. If thickening does not occur after boiling for a few minutes, either add another beaten egg, (don't forget to mix some hot mixture with it first) or add 1 to 2 teaspoons of cornstarch, dissolved in a little water, to the mixture.

3. Always make meringue with the egg whites left from separating eggs for cream and custard pies. Meringue is easy to make and tastes much better than whipped cream.

4. To complement the flavor of your pie, experiment with extracts and flavorings when making meringue. For example, try substituting almond extract, lemon or orange juice, and coconut or buttercream flavoring for vanilla.

5. For a pretty fruit pie, top with a lattice crust instead of a regular crust. On a lightly floured surface, slice a pastry crust into three quarter inch strips to use for lattice work.

6. Use a pie crust shield or thin strips of foil to cover the edges of your pie before baking. This will keep the edges from

becoming over browned. This isn't necessary if you keep a close eye on baking, but in some cases it's better to be safe than sorry.

7. Use firm, ripe fruit in your fruit pies. This applies to apple and fresh pear pies especially. Do not use soft or overripe fruit or your baked pie will resemble sauce more than fruit slices.

8. Cook custard and cream pie filling over low to medium-low heat. Stir constantly as you bring it to a boil to prevent scorching. Custard is ready to use once it is nice and thick, similar in consistency to cooled pudding.

9. When topping a pie with meringue, the meringue should completely cover filling and touch edges of pie shell all the way around.

Pie Crust Recipes

One-Crust Pastry

1 cup all-purpose flour, sifted
½ teaspoon salt
⅓ cup butter or shortening, chilled
2 tablespoons ice water

Combine flour and salt in a bowl. Slowly cut in butter until flour resembles coarse meal. Sprinkle with ice water. Mix to moisten. Form dough into a ball. Chill until ready to use. Roll dough on lightly floured surface or between 2 sheets of waxed paper. Fit dough into center of pie plate. Prick bottom and sides of pastry with a fork. Bake at 450°F (230° C) for 8 to 10 minutes until light brown. Makes one 9-inch crust.

Two-Crust Pastry

2 cups all-purpose flour, sifted
1 teaspoon salt
¾ cup butter or shortening, chilled
4 ½ tablespoons ice water

Combine flour and salt in a bowl. Slowly cut in butter until flour resembles coarse meal. Sprinkle with ice water. Mix to moisten. Form dough into a ball. Chill until ready to use. Divide dough nearly in half. Use the larger portion for the bottom crust. Roll dough on lightly floured surface or between 2 sheets of waxed paper. Fit dough into pie plate. Roll out remaining dough to cover pie filling. Bake as pie recipe requires.

One-Crust Oil Pastry

1 cup all-purpose flour, sifted
2 tablespoons flour, sifted
½ teaspoon salt
⅓ cup vegetable oil, chilled
2 tablespoons ice water

Combine one cup flour, 2 tablespoons flour and salt in a bowl. Add oil. Mix until grainy and flour resembles coarse meal. Sprinkle with ice water. Mix to moisten. Form dough into a ball. Chill until ready to use. Roll dough on lightly floured surface or between 2 sheets of waxed paper. Fit dough into pie plate. Prick bottom and sides of pastry with a fork. Bake at 450°F (230° C) for 12 to 15 minutes until light brown. Makes one 9-inch crust.

Two-Crust Oil Pastry

1 ¾ cups all-purpose flour, sifted
1 teaspoon salt
½ cup vegetable oil, chilled
3 tablespoons ice water

Combine flour and salt in a bowl. Add oil. Mix until grainy and flour resembles coarse meal. Sprinkle with ice water. Mix to moisten. Form dough into a ball. Chill until ready to use. Divide dough nearly in half. Use the larger portion for the bottom crust. Roll dough on lightly floured surface or between 2 sheets of waxed paper. Fit dough into pie plate. Roll out remaining dough to cover pie filling. Bake as pie recipe requires.

Chocolate Wafer Pie Shell (Baked)

1 ½ cups chocolate wafer crumbs (about 33 crushed wafers)
1 ½ tablespoons sugar
⅓ cup butter, melted

Combine crumbs and sugar in a bowl. Stir in butter. Press mixture firmly on bottom and sides of a 9-inch pie plate. Bake at 375°F (190°C) for 8 minutes. Allow to cool before filling.

Gingersnap Pie Shell

1 ½ cups fine gingersnap crumbs (about 30 crushed cookies)
2 tablespoons sugar
5 tablespoons melted butter

Combine crumbs and sugar in a bowl. Stir in butter. Press mixture firmly on bottom and sides of a 9-inch pie plate. Bake at 350°F (180°C) for 8 to 10 minutes until set. Allow to cool before filling.

Graham Cracker Pie Shell (Baked)

1 ½ cups graham cracker crumbs (about 22 crushed graham cracker squares)
⅓ cup sugar
¼ cup butter, melted
¼ teaspoon cinnamon or nutmeg (optional)

Combine crumbs, sugar and spice in a bowl. Stir in butter. Press mixture firmly on bottom and sides of a 9-inch pie plate. Bake at 375°F (190°C) for 8 minutes until light brown. Allow to cool before filling.

Graham Cracker Pie Shell (Unbaked)

1 ½ cups graham cracker crumbs (about 22 crushed graham cracker squares)
⅓ cup sugar
¼ cup butter, melted
¼ teaspoon cinnamon or nutmeg (optional)

Combine crumbs, sugar and spice in a bowl. Stir in butter. Press mixture firmly on bottom and sides of a 9-inch pie plate. Chill until ready to use.

Vanilla Wafer Pie Shell

1 ½ cups vanilla wafer crumbs (about 33 crushed wafers)
1 tablespoon sugar
⅓ cup butter, melted

Combine crumbs and sugar in a bowl. Stir in butter. Press mixture firmly on bottom and sides of a 9-inch pie plate.

Fruit Pie Recipes

Apple Pie

Preheat oven to 425°F (220° C)

Pastry for two-crust pie
5 cups pared, thinly sliced apples
¾ cup sugar
1 tablespoon cornstarch
1 teaspoon apple pie spice
¼ teaspoon salt
2 tablespoons butter or margarine

Line a 9-inch pie plate with pastry. Combine sugar, cornstarch, spice and salt in a bowl. Add apples and toss until coated. Place apple mixture in pie shell. Dot with butter. Cover with top pastry crust. Slit crust and seal edges.

Bake at 425°F for 10 minutes. Reduce temperature to 350°F (180°C) and bake for an additional 35 minutes, or until crust is golden brown.

Apricot Pie

Preheat oven to 425°F (220° C)

Pastry for two-crust pie
1 tablespoon lemon juice
4 cups apricots, seeded, sliced, unpeeled
¾ cup brown sugar
¼ cup sugar
2 tablespoons quick-cooking tapioca
½ teaspoon salt
2 tablespoons butter or margarine

Place apricots in a bowl and sprinkle with lemon juice. In a separate bowl, combine brown sugar, sugar, tapioca and salt. Add to apricots, toss lightly and let stand for 15 minutes. Line a 9-inch pie plate with pastry. Fill with apricot mixture; dot with butter. Cover with top pastry crust. Slit crust and seal edges.

Bake at 425°F for 45 minutes or until medium brown.

Blackberry Pie

Preheat oven to 375°F (190°C)

Pastry for two-crust pie
5 cups fresh or frozen blackberries
1 cup sugar
⅓ cup all-purpose flour
¼ teaspoon salt
2 tablespoons butter or margarine

Line a 9-inch pie plate with pastry. Combine blackberries, sugar, flour and salt in a bowl. Toss until coated. Place blackberry mixture in pie shell. Dot with butter. Cover with top pastry crust. Slit and seal edges.

Bake at 375°F for 45 minutes or until golden brown.

Blueberry Pie

Preheat oven to 375°F (190°C)

Pastry for two-crust pie
4 cups fresh or frozen blueberries
1 cup sugar
¼ cup all-purpose flour
¼ teaspoon salt
¾ teaspoon lemon juice
¼ teaspoon almond extract (optional)
2 tablespoons butter or margarine

Line a 9-inch pie plate with pastry. Combine sugar, flour and salt in a bowl. Add blueberries, lemon juice and almond extract; toss until coated. Place blueberry mixture in pie shell. Dot with butter. Cover with top pastry crust. Slit and seal edges.

Bake at 375°F for 45 minutes or until golden brown.

Cherry Pie

Preheat oven to 425°F (220° C)

Pastry for two-crust pie
16 ounce can pitted red cherries, liquid drained and reserved
2 tablespoons cornstarch
¾ cup sugar
¼ teaspoon salt
1 teaspoon lemon juice
1 tablespoon butter or margarine
¼ teaspoon almond extract

In a pot combine ½ cup cherry liquid, cornstarch, sugar and salt. Cook slowly, stirring constantly until liquid is clear and thick. Add cherries, lemon juice, butter and almond extract. Stir well. Remove from heat and let stand 5 minutes. Line a 9-inch pie plate with pastry. Place cherry mixture in pie shell. Cover with top pastry crust. Slit and seal edges.

Bake at 425°F for 35 to 40 minutes until golden brown.

Cranberry Pie

Preheat oven to 425°F (220° C)

Pastry for two-crust pie
2 cups cranberries, sliced
1 cup raisins, chopped
2 tablespoons all-purpose flour
1 cup sugar
¼ teaspoon salt
½ cup water

Combine cranberries and raisins in a bowl. In a separate bowl, combine flour, sugar and salt. Add to cranberry and raisin mixture. Stir in water and mix well. Line a 9-inch pie plate with pastry. Place mixture in pie shell. Cover with top pastry crust. Slit and seal edges.

Bake at 425°F for 10 minutes. Reduce heat to 350°F (180°C) and bake an additional 30 to 35 minutes until golden brown.

Fresh Cherry Pie

Preheat oven to 425°F (220° C)

Pastry for two-crust pie
4 cups fresh sour cherries, pitted
3 tablespoons quick cooking tapioca
1 cup sugar
¼ teaspoon salt
1 teaspoon lemon juice
¼ teaspoon almond extract

In a bowl combine all ingredients, stir and let stand 15 minutes. Line a 9-inch pie plate with pastry. Place cherry mixture in pie shell. Cover with top pastry crust. Slit crust and seal edges.

Bake at 425°F for 40 to 45 minutes until golden brown.

Peach Pie

Preheat oven to 450°F (230° C)

Pastry for two-crust pie
4 cups sliced, peeled peaches (drain if using canned peaches)
1 tablespoon cornstarch
½ teaspoon salt
½ cup brown sugar
½ cup sugar
1 teaspoon vanilla OR almond extract
1 tablespoon butter or margarine

In a bowl combine cornstarch, salt and sugars. Add peaches and almond extract. Mix well. Line a 9-inch pie plate with pastry. Place peach mixture in pie shell. Cover with top pastry crust. Slit and seal edges.

Bake at 450°F for 10 minutes. Reduce heat to 350°F (180°C) and bake an additional 40 to 50 minutes until golden brown.

Pear Pie

Preheat oven to 450°F (230° C)

Pastry for two-crust pie
5 cups fresh pears, cored, peeled and sliced
½ cup sugar
1 ½ tablespoons quick cooking tapioca
1 teaspoon cinnamon
¼ teaspoon salt
2 teaspoons lemon juice
1 tablespoon butter or margarine

Line a 9-inch pie plate with pastry. Combine sugar, tapioca, spice and salt in a bowl. Layer pear slices in pie plate, sprinkling spice and sugar mixture over each layer. Sprinkle lemon juice over apples. Dot with butter. Cover with top pastry crust. Slit crust and seal edges.

Bake at 450°F for 10 minutes. Reduce temperature to 350°F (180°C) and bake for an additional 35 minutes, or until crust is golden brown.

Raisin Pie

Preheat oven to 425°F (220° C)

Pastry for two-crust pie
2 cups raisins
2 cups boiling water
½ cup sugar
2 tablespoons all-purpose flour
3 tablespoons lemon juice

In a pot combine raising and boiling water. Cover and cook for 5 minutes until tender. Combine sugar and flour in a bowl. Stir into raisins. Cook slowly, stirring constantly, until mixture begins to boil. Boil for one minute. Remove from heat and stir in lemon juice. Pour into pie shell. Cover with top pastry. Slit crust and seal edges.

Bake for 35 to 40 minutes until golden brown.

Rhubarb Pie

Preheat oven to 400°F (200° C)

Pastry for two-crust pie
2 ½ cups rhubarb, cut fine
1 ¼ cups sugar
3 tablespoons all-purpose flour
2 tablespoons butter or margarine

Line a 9-inch pie plate with pastry. Combine sugar and flour in a bowl. Add rhubarb and mix well. Pour into pie shell. Dot with butter. Cover with top pastry. Slit crust and seal edges.

Bake at 400°F for 10 minutes. Reduce heat to 375°F (190°C) and bake for an additional 40 minutes or until golden brown.

Strawberry Pie

9-inch baked pie shell, cooled
6 cups fresh whole strawberries, divided
1 cup sugar
3 tablespoons cornstarch
2 teaspoons lemon juice
¼ teaspoon almond extract
Whipped cream (optional)

Mash 3 cups strawberries in a pot. Add sugar and cornstarch. Cook slowly, stirring constantly, until thick, about 5 minutes. Remove from heat. Stir in lemon juice and almond extract. Let stand to cool. Stir in remaining strawberries.

Pour into baked pie shell. Chill and top with whipped cream, if desired.

Strawberry Rhubarb Pie

Preheat oven to 425° (220° C)

Pastry for two-crust pie
2 cups rhubarb, chopped into 1/4 inch pieces
2 cups strawberries, halved
1 1/4 cups sugar
6 tablespoons all-purpose flour
1 teaspoon vanilla extract
1 teaspoon lemon juice
3 tablespoons butter, cut into pieces

Line a 9-inch pie plate with pastry. In a large bowl combine rhubarb, strawberries, sugar, flour, lemon juice, and vanilla. Mix well and pour into crust. Dot with the butter. Cover with top pastry crust. Slit crust and seal edges. Bake at 425° F 45 to 50 minutes or until filling starts to bubble and crust is golden brown.

Custard Pie Recipes

Butternut Pie

Preheat oven to 450°F (230° C)

Pastry for one-crust pie
½ cup brown sugar
¼ cup sugar
1 tablespoon all-purpose flour
½ teaspoon salt
¾ teaspoon cinnamon
¼ teaspoon ginger
¼ teaspoon nutmeg
¼ teaspoon cloves
1 ½ cups butternut squash, cooked and mashed
1 ½ cups milk
2 eggs, beaten

Line a 9-inch pie plate with pastry. In a large bowl mix sugars, flour, salt and spices together. Add butternut, milk and beaten eggs; stir until smooth. Pour into pie shell.

Bake at 400°F for 10 minutes. Reduce heat to 325°F (170°C) and bake for an additional 30 minutes or until toothpick inserted in center comes out clean.

Butterscotch **Pie**

9-inch baked pie shell
4 tablespoons butter
1 ¼ cups brown sugar
3 tablespoons cornstarch
¼ teaspoon salt
2 cups milk
3 egg yolks, beaten
1 teaspoon vanilla extract

Melt butter in a heavy pot or double boiler. Add brown sugar, cornstarch, and salt. Stir until smooth. Gradually stir in milk. Cook slowly, stirring constantly, until mixture thickens and boils. Boil for 1 minute. Remove from heat. Place egg yolks in a bowl. Stir in ½ sugar mixture. Stir egg mixture into pot. Return to heat and boil for 1 minute. Remove from heat. Stir in vanilla. Pour into baked pie shell.

Top with whipped cream or meringue made from leftover egg whites.

Chess Pie

Preheat oven to 325°F (170°C)

Pastry for one-crust pie
3 eggs, beaten
2 cups brown sugar
2 tablespoons butter or margarine, melted
1 teaspoon vanilla

Line a 9-inch pie plate with pastry. In a medium bowl combine the eggs, sugar, butter and vanilla. Mix well and pour into unbaked pie shell.

Bake 40 to 50 minutes or until toothpick inserted in center comes out clean.

Coconut Custard Pie

9-inch baked pie shell
⅔ cup sugar
3 tablespoons cornstarch
½ teaspoon salt
3 cups milk
2 beaten egg yolks
1 tablespoon butter or margarine
1 ½ teaspoons vanilla extract
1 ½ cups flaked coconut, divided

In a pot combine egg, cornstarch and salt. Gradually stir in milk. Cook slowly, stirring constantly, until mixture thickens and boils. Boil for 1 minute. Remove from heat. Place egg yolks in a bowl. Stir in ½ sugar mixture. Stir egg mixture into sugar mixture in pot. Add ½ cup coconut to pot. Return to heat and boil stirring constantly for 1 minute. Remove from heat. Stir in vanilla, butter and ¾ cup coconut. Pour into baked pie shell.

Custard Pie

Preheat oven to 425°F (220° C)

Pastry for one-crust pie
4 eggs, beaten
½ cup sugar
½ teaspoon salt
2 ½ cups milk
1 teaspoon vanilla extract
Cinnamon, nutmeg or allspice

Line a 9-inch pie plate with pastry. Combine eggs, sugar, salt, milk and vanilla in a bowl. Pour into pie shell. Sprinkle lightly with spice of your choice.

Bake for 30 to 35 minutes or until toothpick inserted in center comes out clean.

Pumpkin Pie

Preheat oven to 450°F (230° C)

Pastry for one-crust pie
¾ cup brown sugar
1 tablespoon all-purpose flour
½ teaspoon salt
¾ teaspoon cinnamon
¼ teaspoon ginger
¼ teaspoon nutmeg
1 ½ cups pumpkin canned pumpkin
1 ½ cups milk
2 large eggs, beaten

Line a 9-inch pie plate with pastry. In a large bowl mix sugar, flour, salt and spices together. Add pumpkin, milk, and beaten eggs; stir until smooth. Pour into pie shell.

Bake at 400°F for 10 minutes. Reduce heat to 325°F (170°C) and bake for an additional 35 to 40 minutes or until toothpick inserted in center comes out clean.

Pumpkin Rum Pie

Preheat oven to 450°F (230° C)

Pastry for one-crust pie
⅔ cup brown sugar
1 tablespoon cornstarch
½ teaspoon salt
1 ½ teaspoons pumpkin pie spice
1 ½ cups pumpkin (canned or mashed)
3 tablespoons rum
1 can evaporated milk (12 ounces)
2 eggs, beaten

Line a 9-inch pie plate with pastry. In a large bowl mix sugar, cornstarch, salt and spice together. Add pumpkin, rum, milk and eggs; stir until smooth. Pour into pie shell.

Bake at 400°F for 10 minutes. Reduce heat to 325°F (170°C) and bake for an additional 35 to 40 minutes or until toothpick inserted in center comes out clean.

Rum Pie

Preheat oven to 425°F (220° C)

Pastry for one-crust pie
4 eggs, beaten
½ cup sugar
½ teaspoon salt
2 ¼ cups milk
¼ cup rum
cinnamon

Line a 9-inch pie plate with pastry. Combine eggs, sugar, salt, milk and rum in a bowl. Pour into pie shell. Sprinkle top lightly with cinnamon.

Bake for 30 to 35 minutes or until toothpick inserted in center comes out clean.

Sweet Potato Pie

Preheat oven to 425°F (220° C)

Pastry for one-crust pie
1 ½ cups mashed sweet potatoes
¼ cup butter or margarine
½ cup brown sugar
½ teaspoon cinnamon
3 eggs
⅓ cup light corn syrup
⅓ cup milk
½ teaspoon salt
1 teaspoon vanilla

Line a 9-inch pie plate with pastry. Cream together butter, sugar and cinnamon. Add mashed sweet potatoes and eggs; stir until blended. Add corn syrup, milk, salt and vanilla. Beat well. Pour into unbaked pie shell.

Bake at 425°F (220° C) for 10 minutes. Reduce heat to 325°F (170°C) and bake for an additional 35 to 45 minutes or until toothpick inserted in center comes out clean.

Cream & Meringue Pies

Banana Cream Pie

9-inch baked pie shell
⅔ cup sugar
3 tablespoons cornstarch
½ teaspoon salt
3 cups milk
3 beaten egg yolks
1 tablespoon butter or margarine
1 ½ teaspoons vanilla extract
3 large bananas, sliced
3 egg whites
6 tablespoons sugar
½ teaspoon vanilla extract

In a pot combine sugar, cornstarch and salt. Gradually stir in milk. Cook slowly, stirring constantly, until mixture thickens and boils. Boil for 1 minute. Remove from heat. Place egg yolks in a bowl. Stir in ½ sugar mixture. Stir egg mixture into sugar mixture in pot. Return to heat and boil stirring constantly for 1 minute. Remove from heat. Stir in vanilla and butter. Line bottom and sides of baked pie shell with banana slices. Pour hot filling into baked pie shell.

For meringue: In a glass or metal bowl whip 3 egg whites until frothy. Gradually beat in 6 tablespoons sugar and ½ teaspoon vanilla. Continue to beat until stiff peaks are formed.

(Banana Cream Pie continued)

Top pie with meringue. Meringue should completely cover filling and touch edges of pie shell. Place in 400°F (200°C) oven and bake 8 to 10 minutes until meringue is lightly browned.

Chocolate Cream Pie

9-inch baked pie shell
1 ½ cups sugar
3 tablespoons cornstarch
½ teaspoon salt
3 cups milk
3 beaten egg yolks
1 tablespoon butter or margarine
1 ½ teaspoons vanilla extract
3 ounces unsweetened chocolate
3 egg whites
6 tablespoons sugar
½ teaspoon vanilla extract

In a pot combine sugar, cornstarch and salt. Gradually stir in milk. Cut up or shave chocolate and add to mixture. Cook slowly, stirring constantly, until mixture thickens and boils. Boil for 1 minute. Remove from heat. Place egg yolks in a bowl. Stir in ½ sugar mixture. Stir egg mixture into sugar mixture in pot. Return to heat and boil stirring constantly for 1 minute. Remove from heat. Stir in vanilla and butter. Pour hot filling into baked pie shell.

(Chocolate Cream Pie continued)

For meringue: In a glass or metal bowl whip 3 egg whites until frothy. Gradually beat in 6 tablespoons sugar and ½ teaspoon vanilla. Continue to beat until stiff peaks are formed.

Top pie with meringue. Meringue should completely cover filling and touch edges of pie shell. Place in 400°F (200°C) oven and bake 8 to 10 minutes until meringue is lightly browned.

Coconut Cream Pie

9-inch baked pie shell
⅔ cup sugar
3 tablespoons cornstarch
½ teaspoon salt
3 cups milk
2 beaten egg yolks
1 tablespoon butter or margarine
1 ½ teaspoons vanilla extract
1 cup flaked coconut, divided
3 egg whites
6 tablespoons sugar
½ teaspoon vanilla extract

In a pot combine sugar, cornstarch and salt. Gradually stir in milk. Cook slowly, stirring constantly, until mixture thickens and boils. Boil for 1 minute. Remove from heat. Place egg yolks in a bowl. Stir in ½ sugar mixture. Stir egg mixture into sugar mixture in pot. Return to heat and boil stirring constantly for 1 minute. Remove from heat. Stir in vanilla, butter and ¾ cup coconut. Pour into baked pie shell.

For meringue: In a glass or metal bowl whip 3 egg whites until frothy. Gradually beat in 6 tablespoons sugar and ½ teaspoon vanilla. Continue to beat until stiff peaks are formed.

Top pie with meringue. Meringue should completely cover filling and touch edges of pie shell. Sprinkle ¼ cup coconut over meringue. Place in 400°F (200°C) oven and bake 8 to 10 minutes until coconut and meringue are lightly browned.

Graham Cracker Cream Pie

9-inch graham cracker pie shell, baked
⅔ cups sugar
3 tablespoons cornstarch
½ teaspoon salt
2 cups milk
3 beaten egg yolks
1 tablespoon butter or margarine
1 ½ teaspoons vanilla extract
¼ cup graham cracker crumbs
3 egg whites
6 tablespoons sugar
½ teaspoon vanilla extract

In a pot combine sugar, cornstarch and salt. Gradually stir in milk. Cook slowly, stirring constantly, until mixture thickens and boils. Boil for 1 minute. Remove from heat. Place egg yolks in a bowl. Stir in ½ sugar mixture. Stir egg mixture into sugar mixture in pot. Return to heat and boil stirring constantly for 1 minute. Remove from heat. Stir in vanilla and butter. Pour hot filling into baked pie shell.

For meringue: In a glass or metal bowl whip 3 egg whites until frothy. Gradually beat in 6 tablespoons sugar and ½ teaspoon vanilla. Continue to beat until stiff peaks are formed.

Top pie with meringue. Meringue should completely cover filling and touch edges of pie shell. Sprinkle graham cracker crumbs on meringue. Place in 400°F (200°C) oven and bake 8 to 10 minutes until meringue is lightly browned.

Lemon Meringue Pie

9-inch baked pie shell
1 ½ cups sugar
⅓ cup cornstarch
½ teaspoon salt
1 ½ cups water
3 beaten egg yolks
3 tablespoon butter or margarine
¼ cup lemon juice
1 tablespoon lemon rind, grated
3 egg whites
6 tablespoons sugar
¼ teaspoon lemon extract

In a pot combine sugar and cornstarch. Gradually stir in water. Cook slowly, stirring constantly, until mixture thickens and boils. Boil for 1 minute. Remove from heat.
Place egg yolks in a bowl. Stir in ½ sugar mixture. Stir egg mixture into sugar mixture in pot. Return to heat and boil stirring constantly for 1 minute longer. Remove from heat. Stir in butter, lemon juice and rind. Blend until smooth. Pour hot filling into baked pie shell.

For meringue: In a glass or metal bowl whip 3 egg whites until frothy. Gradually beat in 6 tablespoons sugar and ¼ teaspoon lemon extract. Continue to beat until stiff peaks are formed.

Top pie with meringue. Meringue should completely cover filling and touch edges of pie shell. Place in 400°F (200°C) oven and bake 8 to 10 minutes until meringue is lightly browned.

Orange Meringue Pie

9-inch baked pie shell
1 cup sugar
⅓ cup cornstarch
½ teaspoon salt
1 ½ cups water
1 ⅓ cups orange juice
3 beaten egg yolks
2 tablespoon butter or margarine
3 egg whites
6 tablespoons sugar
½ teaspoon vanilla extract

In a pot combine sugar and cornstarch. Gradually stir in water. Cook slowly, stirring constantly, until mixture thickens and boils. Boil for 1 minute. Remove from heat. Place egg yolks in a bowl. Stir in ½ sugar mixture. Stir egg mixture into sugar mixture in pot. Return to heat and boil stirring constantly for 1 minute longer. Add orange juice to mixture and boil stirring constantly for 1 additional minute. Mixture should be bubbly and thick. Remove from heat and stir in butter. Blend until smooth. Pour hot filling into baked pie shell.

For meringue: In a glass or metal bowl whip 3 egg whites until frothy. Gradually beat in 6 tablespoons sugar and ½ teaspoon vanilla. Continue to beat until stiff peaks are formed.

Top pie with meringue. Meringue should completely cover filling and touch edges of pie shell. Place in 400°F (200°C) oven and bake 8 to 10 minutes until meringue is lightly browned.

Peach Cream Pie

9-inch baked pie shell
1 egg
1 cup milk
4 tablespoons sugar
2 ½ tablespoons all-purpose flour
¼ teaspoon salt
1 teaspoon vanilla extract
⅓ cup sugar
3 to 4 fresh peaches, pitted, peeled and sliced

Beat egg in a pot. Add milk, 4 tablespoons sugar, flour and salt. Mix well. Cook slowly, stirring constantly, until mixture becomes thick and smooth. Remove from heat. Stir in vanilla. Lightly toss ⅓ cup sugar and fresh peach slices together. Turn into baked pie shell. Cover peach layer with cooked filling. Chill before serving.

Pineapple Cream Pie

9-inch baked pie shell
⅔ cup sugar
3 tablespoons cornstarch
½ teaspoon salt
3 cups milk
3 beaten egg yolks
20 ounce can crushed pineapple, drained
1 tablespoon butter or margarine
1 ½ teaspoons vanilla extract
3 egg whites
6 tablespoons sugar
½ teaspoon vanilla extract

In a pot combine sugar, cornstarch and salt. Gradually stir in milk. Cook slowly, stirring constantly, until mixture thickens and boils. Boil for 1 minute. Remove from heat. Place egg yolks in a bowl. Stir in ½ sugar mixture. Stir egg mixture into sugar mixture in pot. Add pineapple to mixture. Return to heat and boil stirring constantly for 1 minute. Remove from heat. Stir in butter and vanilla. Pour into baked pie shell.

For meringue: In a glass or metal bowl whip 3 egg whites until frothy. Gradually beat in 6 tablespoons sugar and ½ teaspoon vanilla. Continue to beat until stiff peaks are formed.

Top pie with meringue. Meringue should completely cover filling and touch edges of pie shell. Place in 400°F (200°C) oven and bake 8 to 10 minutes until meringue is lightly browned.

Vanilla Cream Pie

9-inch baked pie shell
⅔ cup sugar
3 tablespoons cornstarch
½ teaspoon salt
3 cups milk
3 beaten egg yolks
1 tablespoon butter or margarine
1 ½ teaspoons vanilla extract
3 egg whites
6 tablespoons sugar
½ teaspoon vanilla extract

In a pot combine sugar, cornstarch and salt. Gradually stir in milk. Cook slowly, stirring constantly, until mixture thickens and boils. Boil for 1 minute. Remove from heat. Place egg yolks in a bowl. Stir in ½ sugar mixture. Stir egg mixture into sugar mixture in pot. Return to heat and boil stirring constantly for 1 minute longer. Remove from heat. Stir in vanilla and butter. Pour into baked pie shell.

For meringue: In a glass or metal bowl whip 3 egg whites until frothy. Gradually beat in 6 tablespoons sugar and ½ teaspoon vanilla. Continue to beat until stiff peaks are formed.

Top pie with meringue. Meringue should completely cover filling and touch edges of pie shell. Place in 400°F (200°C) oven and bake 8 to 10 minutes until meringue is lightly browned.

Nut Pies

Black Walnut Pie

Preheat oven to 350°F (180°C)

Pastry for one-crust pie
3 eggs, beaten
1 cup sugar
1 teaspoon vanilla extract
1 cup dark corn syrup
1 cup black walnuts, coarsely chopped

Line a 9-inch pie plate with pastry. Combine all ingredients in a bowl and pour into pie shell. Bake for 45 to 50 minutes or until filling is set.

English Walnut Pie

Preheat oven to Preheat oven to 375°F (190°C)

Pastry for one-crust pie
3 eggs, beaten
⅓ cup sugar
½ teaspoon salt
⅓ cup melted butter
1 cup dark corn syrup
½ teaspoon cinnamon
½ teaspoon nutmeg
½ teaspoon cloves
1 cup English walnuts, coarsely chopped

Line a 9-inch pie plate with pastry. Combine all ingredients except walnuts in a bowl. Beat well. Stir in walnuts and pour into pie shell.

Bake for 40 to 50 minutes or until filling is set.

Macadamia Nut Pie

Preheat oven to 400 (200°C)

Pastry for one-crust pie
½ cup butter or margarine
½ cup brown sugar
1 teaspoon vanilla extract
¼ teaspoon salt
1 cup light corn syrup
3 eggs, beaten
⅔ cup macadamia nuts

Line a 9-inch pie plate with pastry. In a bowl, cream together butter, sugar, vanilla and salt. Stir in syrup and eggs; beat well. Mix in macadamia nuts and pour into pie shell.

Place in 400°F (200°C) oven and bake 10 minutes. Reduce heat to 325°F (170°C) and bake 45 minutes longer or until center is set.

Pecan Pie

Preheat oven to 350°F (180°C)

Pastry for one-crust pie
3 eggs, beaten
1 cup brown sugar
1 teaspoon vanilla extract
1 cup light corn syrup
1 cup pecans, broken or chopped

Line a 9-inch pie plate with pastry. Combine all ingredients in a bowl and pour into pie shell.

Bake for 45 to 50 minutes or until filling is set.

Substitutions

All-purpose flour (1 tablespoon)= ½ tablespoon cornstarch or 2 teaspoons quick-cooking tapioca

Allspice (1 teaspoon)= ½ teaspoon cinnamon, ¼ teaspoon ginger, and ¼ teaspoon cloves

Apple pie spice (1 teaspoon)= ½ teaspoon cinnamon, ¼ teaspoon nutmeg, ⅛ teaspoon allspice, and ⅛ teaspoon cloves

Brown sugar (1 cup, packed)= 1 cup white sugar plus ¼ cup molasses and decrease the liquid in recipe by ¼ cup or 1 cup white sugar or 1 ¼ cups confectioners' sugar

Chocolate square (unsweetened)= 3 tablespoons unsweetened cocoa plus 1 tablespoon shortening or vegetable oil

Cocoa (¼ cup)= 1 (1-ounce) square unsweetened chocolate

Cornstarch (1 tablespoon)= 2 tablespoons all-purpose flour or 1 ⅓ tablespoons quick-cooking tapioca

Corn syrup (1 cup)= 1 ¼ cup white sugar plus ⅓ cup water or 1 cup honey

Lemon juice (1 teaspoon)= ½ teaspoon vinegar or 1 teaspoon white wine or 1 teaspoon lime juice

Macadamia nuts (1 cup)= 1 cup almonds or 1 cup hazelnuts

Pumpkin pie spice (1 teaspoon)= ½ teaspoon cinnamon, ⅛ teaspoon cloves, ¼ teaspoon ginger, and ⅛ teaspoon nutmeg

Tapioca (1 tablespoon quick-cooking)= 1 ½ tablespoon of all-purpose flour or ½ tablespoon cornstarch

White sugar (1 cup)= 1 cup brown sugar or 1 ¼ cups confectioners' sugar or ¾ cup honey or ¾ cup corn syrup

NOTES

NOTES

Made in the USA
Monee, IL
08 July 2026

56715876R00037